A More Excellent Way

A Commentary on the World Today /
Loving God and Your Neighbor

Jim Dickson

A More Excellent Way

A Commentary on the World Today /
Loving God and Your Neighbor

Table of Contents

Introduction

Writing this commentary began in early spring. At that time branches were bare on the birch tree outside my window. Now there are newly minted green leaves fluttering in the breeze. I thought, "This is the opposite of Covid-19." Two months ago life was good and we were looking forward with great enthusiasm for the coming of spring. Now there is a "bareness" to life. The pandemic has left our world devoid of many of the close relationships and activities that brought happiness to everyday living. How do we get back to life that is fun, fulfilling, and meaningful? That is the purpose of "*A More Excellent Way.*"

This commentary is the last of an "unplanned" trilogy written by the author, unplanned because as events in the world changed it was evident that additional commentaries were needed. The first *Mere Humanity* grew out of an awareness that loneliness is a significant problem in our culture and is often related to self-centeredness, anger, and divisiveness.

A summary of the book might be helpful. The commentary began with the story of man's creation and explored the essence of man and our dual good and bad natures, good coming from being made in the image of God; bad the result of disobedience in the Garden of Eden. An understanding of our dual human natures provides an answer to the questions of "Why do we do what we do not want to do?" and "Why do we not do what we want to do?" The commentary concluded that the answer was to "love

God and love your neighbor[1] also known as The Greatest Commandment.

The Covid-19 disaster followed soon after that commentary was published and resulted in a 2nd commentary *Why Disasters*. It discussed disasters over the history of man and led to a finding that disasters and man's disobedience were frequently, although not always, interrelated. A search for how we should deal with disasters led to the Founding Fathers' model and motto for how to deal with their disaster, the Revolutionary War. "United we stand, divided we fall!" This in turn gave birth to a new way for a nation to govern itself—a government of the people, by the people, and for the people. Although diverse in education,

---

[1] Jesus replied: " 'Love the Lord your God with all your heart and with all your soul and with all your mind.' This is the first and greatest commandment. And the second is like it: 'Love your neighbor as yourself.' All the Law and the Prophets hang on these two commandments." Matthew 22:37-40 NIV

ages, occupations, and beliefs the Founders rose above their differences and bonded to solve their common problems. They were living out the greatest commandment. In doing so they built a solid foundation for this nation to become over time the most admired country in the world.

The trilogy deals with loneliness, disasters, and now disarray. All three are malfunctions that are involved in one way or another with man's inner condition. Evil in the heart can lead to aloneness; a felt need to break rules relating to right and wrong can lead to retribution; an unwillingness to cooperate is a strong barrier to progress. Since all three conditions flow out of a common source, self-centeredness, it should not be surprising that they have a common solution—love.

Love is a subject unlike any other, but it will be discussed in this commentary primarily as it relates to the Greatest Commandment. Before discussing a solution however it will be wise to understand the situation we face today. It is sobering. The times call for a dramatic change in how we live. We have been captivated by materialism but have abandoned wonderment. The former can give immediate pleasure but rarely gives more than temporary satisfaction. The latter goes below the surface and energizes qualities that distinguish man from animal and raises deep-seated questions such as who am I, why was I created, and how do I fit in to the whole of creation? Transcendent living creates a desire to serve creation rather than have it serve ourselves.

We have gotten off track, big time. We are living in a culture of violence. Brutality by a few is condemned by otherwise peaceful citizens who then themselves engage in violence. The result is a vicious circle. Common sense suggests the alternate is a solution based on peacefulness. The purpose of this commentary, *A More Excellent Way* is to show how fallen man can use Covid-19 as an inspiration to make loving God and man normal living. But first, what is going on?

Dismay

What is going on is dismay. This is a fitting phrase for today. In 1776 British citizen Thomas Paine said, *"These are time that try men's souls."* He was referring to the challenges the colonists faced as the Revolutionary War began. The future was uncertain but what was certain to Paine was that the cause was just and there needed to be a clear statement of the abuses that the colonists felt were unjust. He did so in a way that united his new country. It is said his writing, *Common Sense*, was the single most powerful force that united the colonies. A clear understanding of the abuses that came from the King and parliament was a key factor in uniting the colonists to successfully achieve independence.

We are again at war but this time it is against the force of a mighty virus. Covid-19 has physically, socially, and economically interrupted the normal flow of life worldwide. It is damaging in countless ways. Just as in Paine's time, it is once again important to have a clear understanding of the root problem that is causing the disaster. Why do we have the problem, and what is necessary in order for the people to unite to defeat the enemy. Federal, state, and local government officials are emphasizing the importance of protective action and efforts are being made to produce a vaccine that will minimize the impact of this "enemy." These however do not deal with the root question: What gave birth to this virus?

Natural disasters, so-called acts of God such as plagues, make it much more difficult to answer the question of what caused the cause that caused the damage? We can see the damage. We know it was caused by a virus. But what brought the virus into existence? Efforts are being made to pinpoint where and how the virus was released. But what caused the virus to be in existence? This proposition was examined in the book *Why Disaster* with the conclusion that so-called Acts of God can be a product of man's actions. We use the phrase "Acts of God" as a label for actions that seem to be beyond the realm of reason. However since the word "God" is commonly brought into the equation in discussing certain disasters, it would seem reasonable to examine whether God might in fact be a factor in causing "Acts of God."

The commentary *Why Disaster* contained a "Lax List"[2] of spiritual activities done, or left undone. They are activities that are man's agenda and contrary to God's agenda. They are matters involving man's conduct that have been a focal point of fighting between Satan and God's people through the ages but especially in the past 60 years. It is logical to ask why those matters were felt to be appropriate.

In his Introduction to the 3rd edition of *Common Sense*, Paine wrote, "*a long habit of not thinking a thing WRONG, gives it a superficial appearance of being RIGHT, and raises at first a formidable outcry in defense of custom. But the tumult soon subsides.*"

Could it be that for a long time we have been doing some things that are WRONG that we now assume they

---

[2] See Appendix.

are RIGHT, but we are unaware they are the cause of disaster?

Could it be that we *accept* disasters as a normal part of the way the world functions instead of searching for root causes?

Could it be that we have come to believe how we *now* live and move and have our being is what is RIGHT even though it is contrary to God's agenda?

Could it be that we are governed by natural laws that show the RIGHT direction to go on many major issues but on which we are going in the opposite direction, the WRONG direction?

Could it be that the foundation the Founders established for this country is RIGHT but what we as a people *want* today is WRONG even though it is slowly replacing the Founders' foundation?

Could it be that the loneliness, anger, divisiveness, and self-centeredness rampant in our culture today is the result of *moving off* the foundation the Founders built?

The above are questions that are explored in *A More Excellent Way*. Commentaries are often written to stimulate thinking and include propositions to be discussed in addition to being a source of answers. We hope you find both questions and answers in this writing and we encourage you to find others with whom you can discuss your questions and share your answers.

Now it is time to move from dismay to disarray! This will enable us to understand the *cause* that caused Covid-19.

Disarray

Our country is in disarray. The disarray had been going on for fifty or more years and has been gradually getting worse. Now Covid-19 has brought the country to a near standstill, but perhaps this is a blessing. The virus can serve as a time-out and get people to reflect on:

- Look at the mess we are in.
- How did this happen?[3]
- What have we done to ourselves?
- What happened to the land of the free and the home of the brave?

No single word can effectively describe the situation in our nation today, but it is

---

[3] An ageless question. Over 3,000 years ago in the era of Judges, Gideon asked, *"But if the Lord is with us, why has all this happened to us?"* See Judges 6:13.

a hodgepodge of self-centeredness, materialism, lack of direction, elusive search for happiness, discrimination, loneliness, broken relationships, arrogance, and following the wrong agenda.

Pick up a paper any day or tune on radio or TV. The damage from activity, or lack thereof, will jump out at you. Statues of leaders who contributed to the greatness of this country, despite flaws, are being torn down. Congressmen can't even agree to discuss police reform although law enforcement *modus operandi* is the core of riots in many cities. Similarly alternate ways of structuring school systems never make it to the floor for debate by legislators. Immigration reform is anathema to many despite mutual agreement on the need for change.

Here is an example. Our state university system has been searching for a new president for a long while. Consultant fees exceed two hundred thousand dollars and many candidates were interviewed but withdrew, including the finalist who said, "I appreciate the strong support from the search committee… but it's clear they have important process issues to work out."

Major league baseball owners and players live lives that are the envy of many. Everyone likes games, but only a lucky few get to play games for a living (or manage sports organizations). The seasons are short, the pay is enormous, and the people involved by and large are the cream of the crop. Who wouldn't want to keep that good thing going? Yet the season delayed by Covid-19 involved "bitter haggling between player and owners over money."[4] Fruitless negotiations, wasted time, delayed results. Baseball also has "important process issues to work out."

---

[4] Milwaukee *Journal*, sec.1b, June 29, 2020

18

Readers and listeners to the media can add their own stories to this stew of unresolved problems that won't go away. They increase daily in number and intensity. Unresolved problems lead to activity with only marginal results and frustration for everyone. Over and over there are "important process issues to work out."

What is the root of these problems, this disarray? All involve relationships, the core of any "people" activity including marriage, home, community, education, business, non-profits, and government. Everyone has an ego. Every ego has a self-will that has its own agenda. Getting egos to focus on what is right rather then who is right is a critical factor in effectiveness in making things work. Relationships that work are akin to a well-oiled machine with all parts working in unison for a common goal. When relationships are fractured everything can become an issue and an insurmountable barrier.

On the international scene, two recent books by Kim Ghattis are informative and thought-provoking regarding relationships. The first book, *The Secretary*, tells of her traveling as a BBC correspondent with Secretary of State Hillary Clinton. Ghattis was born and raised in Lebanon and her details of the undercurrents of the Middle East politics are exceptional. Her second book *Black Wave* published in 2020 discusses events over the past 40 years in seven of the most prominent Middle East countries. Her detailed writing of changes (or lack of change) in that region in 10 years are classic. Words and phrases used by reviewers of the book to describe the era and region include "destructive rivalry," "pernicious effect," "dark age," "curtain of violence," "blackness," and "consequential contests threatening global security." What stands out in the book are the fractured relationships that in turn led to constant disarray in individual countries and in the region.

A second example of fractured relationships is the U.S. Congress: qualified individuals, by and large; near unlimited resources; a strong tradition of a government "of the people, by the people and for the people." But today a better description is government by the government for those elected to govern. For the past 20 years one of most admired countries in the world can't get its act together to balance a budget. The emphasis on who is right rather than agreeing on what is right has created a monster with an insatiable appetite.

Pick a subject, and the cost of not cooperating stands out. U.S./China relations regularly face serious bumps in the road, often at great cost to various groups in both countries including large and small businesses and agriculture. Nearer to home, how long did it take to redo a trade deal with Mexico and Canada? Too long. These are inconsequential compared to the cost of lives in tribal wars in various parts of the world by leaders striving for control rather than cooperation.

Back in this country at the grass roots level things are no different. We are no longer *"One nation, indivisible with liberty and justice for all."* Our pledge of allegiance and flag designed to unite the three hundred fifty million citizens of the country does everything but unite. Football players, fans, flag burners, and protesters seize opportunities to hype their cause, too often on occasions where the original intent was to promote oneness. What does it take to unite?

The Great Depression unified. Neighbors helping neighbors was everywhere evident in that grim decade when neighboring was the norm more than any other time in the previous hundred years. Wars unite, especially when the war is the response to an attack. The 1950s were a time of neighbors helping neighbors after the trials of the 30's and 40's.

There is a glow of goodness in people that needs a reason to reignite. Covid-19 has brought out a degree of caring and kindness though it is primarily confined to those on the front lines, people caring for suffering people. Public health and safety workers, the overwhelming number of whom seek liberty and justice for all, are too often the targets of those suffering from the results of fractured relationships.

A model of citizens living out their pledge of allegiance is needed. For that we need to go back nearly 250 years. The Founders of our great nation gave it to us. We need to re-examine our roots.

Hooray

How to go from disarray to hooray? In this chapter we will discuss the activities and beliefs of the Founding Fathers because they did it, they went from disorder to hooray! They went from being thirteen independent colonies to being one united nation. In addition it became a much-needed model for the world of a government that existed to serve the people, a model we need to heed today.

The collection of leaders who came together in 1775 to declare independence and bring a new nation into being gave the world a model for government that has never been surpassed. The model was set out in its Declaration of Independence that stated,

> *We hold these truths to be self-evident, that all men are created equal, that they are endowed by their Creator with certain unalienable Rights, that among these are Life, Liberty and the pursuit of Happiness. That to secure these right, Governments are instituted among Men, deriving their just powers from the consent of the governed.*

There is much that is remarkable about this statement.

There are *truths* and they are self-evident, not something man just thought up;

The truths are *self-evident*, undisputable;

The truths come from a Creator; they were not something bestowed by man;

Men were created *equal,* no more kings by divine right;

Man was a *creation,* the work of a Creator, not a random product of evolution;

Rights are unalienable; they can't be taken away; and

Governmental power comes from *consent* of the people.

Before discussing the subject matter of this statement it would be very helpful to determine why the Founders felt as they did about the truths they were building into the nation's government. Where did the "truths" come from? Where did they originate?

A clue is the lead-in paragraph of the Declaration of Independence that affirmed that there are "Laws of Nature and of Nature's God."[5] The Founders sought to build a nation on the laws of nature and nature's God. This is a phrase found frequently in writings at that time. There is disagreement today as to the meaning of this phrase, but research shows that the Founders were searching for common ground, and they found it in the laws of nature and nature's God. They didn't just put together what they felt was right. They found it in their belief in a supreme being who was the God of nature. They saw order in nature and their research showed that order came from nature's God. They wanted order, and they found it.

A scholarly treatment of "Laws of Nature and of Nature's God" appears in a recent article by Kerry L Morgan titled

---

[5] The topic "Laws of Nature and of Nature's God" is included in this commentary primarily to emphasize the role it played in uniting the Founders.

The True Foundation of American Law.[6] The article includes a statement by John Quincy Adams that the framers of the Constitution were in one accord in *"pre-suppose(ing) the existence of a God, the moral ruler of the universe, and a rule of right and wrong, of just and unjust, binding upon man, preceding all institution of human society and government."*

In the Declaration of Independence the Founders started with truths that had existed through the ages. They labeled these as self-evident. When it came time to write a Constitution some ten years later it was natural for the writers of that document[7] to work from these "self-evident truths" and write a preamble that naturally flowed from the Declaration's statements, especially the statement that

---

[6] https://lonang.com/commentaries/conlaw/organizing/laws-of-nature-and-natures-god/

[7] There were 56 men who signed the Declaration and 39 who signed the Constitution but only 6 signed both documents. For simplicity this commentary uses "Founders" to refer to both group as they all were part of the process of "making order out of chaos" and of uniting the states.

all men are created equal and have un-alienable rights.

> **We the People** *of the United States, in Order to form a more perfect Union, establish Justice, insure domestic* **Tranquility**, *provide for the common defence, promote the general Welfare, and secure the Blessings of Liberty to ourselves and our Posterity, do ordain and establish this Constitution for the United States of America.*

The Founders in their wisdom didn't feel it was important to come to agreement on the exact nature of this supreme being called by various names including God, the Creator, and Providence but there was no significant disagreement that there was a God who was supreme.

As noted previously the Founders were a diverse group with strong conflicting beliefs on significant matters (e.g. religion and slavery), but near unanimous in the belief in God. Their common spiritual bond provided respect for one another, enabled them to rise above self-interest, and opened their hearts and minds to the thoughts and ideas of others. A sample of quotes reveal the source of their respect[8].

> Patrick Henry: *"An appeal to arms and the God of hosts is all that is left us. But we shall not fight our battle alone. There is a just God that presides over the destinies of nations. I know not what course others may take, but as for me, give me liberty, or give me death."*

> John Jay, our first Supreme Court Justice stated *"when we select our national leaders, if we are to preserve our Nation, we must select Christians. Providence has given to our people the choice of their rulers and it is the duty as well as*

---

[8] The Founders' varied in their understanding of the higher power and what it meant to be a "Christian." Nonetheless the differences weren't a barrier to unity.

the privilege and interest of our Christian Nation to select and prefer Christians for their rulers."

Washington's General Orders, November 27, 1779: *"Whereas it becomes us humbly to approach the throne of Almighty God, with gratitude and praise for the wonders which his goodness has wrought in conducting our fore-fathers to this western world...and above all, that he hath diffused the glorious light of the gospel, whereby, through the merits of our gracious Redeemer, we may become the heirs of his eternal glory."*

Washington in a letter to Rev. William Gordon, May 13, 1776 also had a strong reliance on the divine: *"No man has a more perfect Reliance on the alwise (sic) and powerful dispensations of the Supreme Being than I have nor thinks his aid more necessary."*

John Adams in an address to military leaders. *"Our constitution was made only for a moral and religious people. It is wholly inadequate to the government of any other."*

Thirty years later John Quincy Adams, 6th president and son of John Adams said, *"The highest glory of the American Revolution was this: it connected in one indissoluble bond the principles of civil government with the principles of Christianity."*

Thomas Jefferson wrote on the front of his well-worn Bible: *'I am a Christian, that is to say a disciple of the doctrines of Jesus. I have little doubt that our whole country will soon be rallied to the unity of our Creator and, I hope, to the pure doctrine of Jesus also."*

Benjamin Franklin in a letter to President of Yale: *'Here is my Creed. I believe in one God, Creator of the Universe. That he governs it by his Providence. That he ought to be worshipped.*

In passing it should be noted that when Franklin was asked what kind of government we will have, he answered, *A republic, if you can keep it.* He obviously had a premonition that there would be strong temptations and ongoing battles in government and among the populace to use the instrument of government to make decisions for the benefit of a few instead of government for the benefit of the people. This is the battle we are in today.

The Founders shared belief in God enabled them to rise above the trenches of "what I want" and breath in the rarified air of "what is right." By and large they were of one mind when it came to solving problems.

The Founders also found unity in their frequent reference to the Bible. This is a topic that deserves separate treatment but it is sufficient here to note Washington's Thanksgiving Proclamation of 1795. It contained a litany of blessings and stated that their continuance depends in some way upon our fulfilling *"our many and great obligations to the Almighty."*

There is a major misunderstanding of the Constitution today in regard to the Bible and similar writings. The Founders were careful not to single out the Bible as the religion of the nation, but they made it clear the Constitution does *not forbid* reference to the Bible. It simply says, *"Congress shall make no law respecting an establishment of religion, or prohibiting the exercise thereof."* Using words or phrases from the Bible is not making a *"law respecting an establishment of religion."*

A built-in trust is essential for solving problems. The Founders had trust through their common spiritual beliefs. This made it possible to have a natural flow of both telling and hearing by both parties. Writings from that time including the Federalist Papers[9] are rich in giving the viewpoints of varied parties and long discussions until there was agreement and a solution. There were thorny issues. Large states, and there were several, did not want small states to have equal representation in the senate. There were disagreements on assuming wartime debts of the continental congress, major differences over the power of the central government and especially on powers of the chief executive.

However, what is happening today is that truths the Founders built into the foundation of the nation are being muted by courts while falsehoods on the

---

[9] A series of 85 essays written by Alexander Hamilton, John Jay, and James Madison between October 1787 and May 1788. The essays were published anonymously, under the pen name "Publius." For full text see: https://guides.loc.gov/federalist-papers/full-text

same subject are being held up as truths.[10] Historian Robert R. Reilly recently stated,

"As soon as one moves from the rational 'Laws of Nature and of Nature's God' to the one making human will that standard, one is headed for Leviathan. We are now enduring such a transformation in the United States where political rule is becoming increasingly arbitrary."

Thomas Paine's warning is still appropriate, *"A long habit of not thinking a thing WRONG, gives it a superficial appearance of being RIGHT."*

What is the lesson we can learn from the Founders to reverse this distortion of the Founders intent? This will be briefly covered in the next section, "It Will Be Hard." First some examples of the very

---

[10] America on Trial, in Defense of the Founding, Ignatius Press 2020, p. 317

thing Paine warned against. Today we call this political correctness.

Occasionally I write a Letter to the Editor on issues I feel are under-reported. My letter raised the question of whether Covid-19 might be God's retribution for our disobedience on a variety of social issues. The letter was initially accepted but later rejected by the editor. When I asked for the reason I was told my letter was one-sided. I said that was the point, your paper is consistently one-sided on this issue; none of the other letters on Covid-19 even hinted at the possibility that, like in Noah's time, God is trying to get our attention.

A recent national example of the trend away from the Founder's beliefs occurred in May at graduation time. Since schools would not be hearing graduation speakers this year because of Covid-19 restrictions, a leading national newspaper asked twenty prominent (non-political) leaders of our country to submit articles giving advice to graduates. The responses were published in a separate section of the paper devoted just to this topic. Individually all the responses were worthy. But all dealt with secular matters. Not one included a word, sentence, or paragraph of a spiritual nature. My thoughts went back to the Founders and to Washington in the war for independence. How would they have fought if all they were given was man's wisdom, without wisdom and power from on high? What a sad commentary on our country today that so many prestigious leaders would fail to include any advice of a spiritual nature for those who would be soon be leaving the world of education and taking on responsibility for the welfare of our nation and culture.

What now have we learned?

   o We have a nation with a solid foundation built on truths set out in the Declaration of Independence, the Constitution, and the Laws of Nature and Nature's God.

o We have a Constitution that provides for the free exercise of religion, and freedom of speech, press and assembly.

o We have a warning that through silence that which is WRONG can be perceived as RIGHT.

o We have the Founder's example of a bond that transcended difference and enabled them to focus on God's agenda.

o We have the Founder's rich examples of how to communicate on issues on which a culture is in disarray, and then engage in deliberations that lead to truths.

Now to be informed regarding obstacles to achieve common goals and why it will be difficult.

It Will be Difficult

How do we go from disarray to "hooray" as our Founders did? We have the advantage of their model that enabled them to go from the disarray of the Revolutionary War to independence. Their model worked well for over two centuries, but now we are going in the opposite direction. We must change directions, but before discussing how we might do that it would be beneficial to make an honest assessment of our present condition for we as a nation are currently in denial similar to the condition of people who suffer from an addiction.

The Founders recognized that "Nature's Laws and the Laws of God's nature" were God's agenda taken from scripture and that disobedience can lead to retribution. The *Lax List* in the appendix covers a variety of areas in which disobedience to scriptural teachings today is the norm. Note that the Founders in their wisdom did not make specific laws that would cover many of these areas, such as church attendance and tithing. This would have resulted in legalism, "You have to do this," rather than "You ought to do this? The former leads to bondage; the latter leads to freedom and makes loving relationship possible.

Recovering from our addictions to going our way rather than the Creator's way will be difficult for a litany of reasons:

> Habits are *hard to change*, especially those imbedded in genes we received from our ancestor Adam.

The subject matter of the solution; love, is amorphous, formless, fluid and therefore *hard to comprehend*.

The subject matter involves *emotions* that tend to mess with reasoning.

The word "love" encompasses a variety of thoughts, actions, and emotions that can have *different meanings* in secular and sacred worlds.

There are few *living examples* to point to and say, "This is what the world would be like if we loved God and our neighbor."

A standard, like "greatest" as in "The Greatest Commandment" is an *uncomfortable standard* that people resist.

The word "commandment" has a *negative connotation* that impedes reasoning.

The secular world *resists discussions* of a spiritual nature.

Christians do not have a good record of *communicating spiritual truths* to the secular world.

God's unselfish love is *threatening* to self-will, one of man's prized possessions.

In summary, the *world is too much with* us.

An analogy might be helpful. Assume the owner of a large organization appointed someone to manage his/her affairs and then left for an extended period of time. The owner provided resources, an agenda, and instructions on what was to be done. Assume that the owner came back but found the caretaker had *substituted* his agenda and ways of doing things, and the results were the opposite of what the owner had communicated. What would he do?

This is the Genesis story of early man in the Garden of Eden. Later God sent a flood to wipe out all his creation except Noah and his family. The Old Testament contains many other stories of man's disobedience and God's retribution, stories of disobedience and disaster.

Today man has substituted his power and pleasure agenda for God's agenda. God's agenda is for man and woman to marry and to *"Be fruitful and increase in number; fill the earth and subdue it"*[11] is distorted. His instructions in the Greatest Commandment to love God and your neighbor is given only lukewarm obedience. His Ten Commandments are seldom quoted and often violated.

Following God's agenda is not easy. Items in the Lax List are evidence of how difficult it is. However we have the Founders model and we would do well to follow it. They didn't try to invent the wheel. They studied governments of other civilization going back to England, France, Rome, Jerusalem, and the early Greek experience with a democracy. The

---

[11] *Genesis 1:27-28*

result was a Constitution that incorporated wisdom from the ages in determining right and wrong.

A major problem today is secular forces have gradually changed the original meaning of the Constitution to reflect the will of people today. In doing so right and wrong based on "laws of nature's God" is being turned around from what the Founders intended and ignoring that not doing what is right can lead to disasters—like Covid-19.

The preamble to the Constitution captured the founders vision of what is right:

> *We the People of the United States, in Order to form a <u>more perfect Union</u>, establish Justice, insure <u>domestic Tranquility</u>, provide for the <u>common defence</u>, promote the <u>general Welfare</u>, and secure the <u>Blessings of Liberty</u> to ourselves and our Posterity, do ordain*

and establish this Constitution for the United States of America. [emphasis added]

It is the Creator's agenda for all creation; "perfect union," "tranquility," "common defense," "welfare," "blessings," "liberty." Our question now is what is required to make this a reality? But first a pause.

Pause

What is the situation in our nation today?

Covid-19, no matter the cause, has forced us to re-examine *how we relate* to one another.

The present situation in our country is *intolerable*. Disarray and frustration abound.

Frustration resulting from unresolved problems has resulted in rampant *domestic terrorism*.

Problem solving requires a *process* but people are unwilling to join in such a process, a situation Benjamin Franklin warned against, "*A republic if you can keep it.*"

Problem solving processes require respect for others and a willingness to value *what* is right over *who* is right.

The root problem, man's self-centered *old nature,* is widespread.

The Founders reliance on "*the laws of nature and nature's God*" provides a common bond for over-riding self-interest.

A s*pirituality* is lacking in our culture today.

Change will be difficult because it means saying no to self-will.

The Creator saw our addiction and knew we would need help so he provided a "secret sauce."

Secret Sauce

What is the secret sauce that the Creator provided for a time such as this? It is the provision God provided when he created man in His image. It is the provision the Founders relied on to smooth out their differences when seeking their common good. (The Founders still quarreled but unity prevailed because the secret sauce reigned.)

An analogy might help to understand secret sauce. How popular is spinach? Have you ever heard someone say, "I hope we have spinach for dinner tonight"? Have you seen spinach listed as a "side" to order with a dinner in a restaurant? Probably not. Spinach is out of favor.

My wife has a recipe for spinach salad that involves a secret salad dressing. She makes spinach salad several times a year when we have an excess of spinach from our garden. I would normally never ask for spinach, but her spinach salad with a secret sauce is delicious and invariably brings out my comment, "What makes this so good?" The reply, "The salad dressing recipe the chef at (a Milwaukee restaurant) gave me several years ago." My consistent answer, "I don't like spinach, but I love this salad." The secret sauce from a master chef made all the difference.

The Creator provides a "secret sauce." It is called love. How good is this "secret sauce"? He called it the greatest commandment![12] It never fails, blesses both giver and receiver, and is available for

---

[12] See Introduction p.1 footnote

the asking. It is his ultimate resource to restore a heaven-to-earth relationship with man and to make possible loving human relationships on earth.

God's word gives us the ingredients that make up of his "secret sauce."

> *Love is patient, love is kind. It does not envy, it does not boast, it is not proud. It does not dishonor others, it is not self-seeking, it is not easily angered, it keeps no record of wrongs. Love does not delight in evil but rejoices with the truth. It always protects, always trusts, always hopes, always perseveres. Love never fails.*[13]

To understand why this secret sauce is not the norm today we need to remember that in the Garden of Eden our ancestor Adam and Eve chose to obey Satan. They found his promise *"when you eat of (the apple) your eyes will be opened and*

---

[13] 1 Corinthians 13:5-8 NIV

52

you will be like God"[14] irresistible. The result was sin, separation from God. The result also meant that today we are part of the 8 billion gods on earth who have Satan's sin nature along-side our "image of God" nature, and they are constantly battling to be number one. No wonder the country is in disarray.

God's gift of love has always been available as an antidote to override our evil nature, our desire to be #1. Choosing to be loving enables us to have oneness with God and with our "neighbor"[15]. Having oneness with God, Creator of heaven and earth, is a value beyond measure.

It is no surprise that God said the greatest commandment is to love him and our neighbor. Love is essential for lasting relationships. Fortunately the Creator

---

[14] See Genesis 3:5

[15] See the parable in Luke 10:29-36 on who is our neighbor. A common interpretation, anyone with a need that God brings into our lives.

has an unlimited supply. He knew we would need it. Even more amazing, the only cost is trade our way for his way. Trading our way for God's way is not easy. Our self-centeredness does not like to be dependent on anyone, but it is a small price to give up garbage for glory.

The word "love" has many meanings.[16] Unfortunately our culture has not done a good job of distinguishing the various kinds of love. (A case can be made that Satan, the great deceiver, had a hand in this to spread confusion).

Another difficulty arises in matters involving both love and reason, and there are many. Love primarily involves faith and feeling, matters of the heart; reason primarily involves logic and thinking, matters of the head. One could say love and reason are in two different worlds. It is not easy finding common ground on

---

[16] It is worth noting that the word "love" is both a noun that refers to something specific and a verb that connotes action.

issues that involve both. However both head and heart come from the Creator. He can provide balance if we seek his will. Reason and feeling are not meant to be opposites but are designed to blend in order to avoid the perils of extremes, and to achieve a more excellent way.

The word "love" calls for astute insight. Various languages list from three to eight different types of love, and not all are good. The problems is compounded because, to paraphrase Paine, when we use the wrong meaning of a word for a long period of time it becomes the right meaning. The word love in our culture has been convoluted.

In Greek (the language of the New Testament), four different words are used for "love":

> *Eros*: Sexual or romantic love. It is powerful. It is a gift from God when used properly; a tool of Satan when abused.

Philia: Affection for family, close friends, and team members. Philia love provides the stability needed cultural bonding.

Familia: Deep affection for family members, including extended family. This love also provides cultural stability especially for passing on spiritual truths and values.

Agape: wholesome, unconditional love that God has for man and man has for God.

This commentary primarily has to do with *agape* love. It is the secret sauce that gave the Founders power from on high needed for unity.

Agape love for individuals is analogous to what gasoline is for vehicles. It isn't complicated to use, exists in abundance, and is powerful. A major difference, people generally fill up with gasoline before the tank gets empty; we often delay, seek other answer, and procrastinate before making the transition from "what I want" to "how can I help my neighbor."

It is helpful to have a clear picture of benefits that result from "loving our neighbor" because our self resists sharing authority. The Founders provided a guide to the benefits they felt were important. They are embodied in the Preamble to the Constitution:

> *"A more perfect union, justice, domestic tranquility, common defense, promotion of the general welfare, blessings of liberty now and to our posterity."*

That is a powerful vision and it provided a solid foundation for the colonies to become the United States of America. It is sad to compare the disarray in our country today with the unity the Founders achieved.

We have largely gone in the opposite direction from the Preamble for scores of years. As covered in *Why Disasters*, disobedience has consequences. Why should we be surprised that Covid-19 has brought the nation to a crippling slow down?

The critical question now is "What must we do?" The obvious answer is, be obedient, starting with the greatest commandment. To be more loving we must return, as the Founders did, to the source of love, the one who commanded us to, *"Love the Lord your God with all your heart and with all your soul and with all your strength."*[17]

How to be obedient to this commandment is covered in the next section, Transformation. It will be difficult; "who knows but that we have come to our position for such a time as this?"[18]

---

[17] Deuteronomy 6:5 NIV
[18] Esther 4:14 paraphrased

Transformation

Background

At Creation God **formed** the world, made man and woman, told them to multiply and fill the earth, and said that the Greatest Commandment was to love him and our neighbors.

Two thousand years ago God sent his son to make disciples to **transform** the world. They were instructed to *"go make disciples of all nations"* who would *"observe all his commandments."* His son's death freed disciples from the bondage of sin and made Holy Spirit power available by accepting Jesus Christ as Lord and Savior.

Two hundred and fifty years ago our Founders used His power to pledge their lives, fortunes and sacred honor to **transform** government from sovereign rule to rule of, by, and for the people.

In the Civil War one hundred and fifty years ago, 600,000 men were casualties to avoid **transformation**. Lincoln said, *"That this nation under God might have a new birth of freedom and that government of the people, by the people and for the people shall not perish from the earth."*[19]

Today

We are in a battle against a mighty foe, Covid-19. Could it be that this is the consequence of disobedience? The late Warren Wiersbe, noted Christian teacher and former pastor of Moody Bible Church in his 1996 book *Be Amazed* discussed "Day of the Lord" and God's in-

---

[19] Abraham Lincoln, Gettysburg address, Nov. 19, 1863

60

tervention in worldly affairs. He stated, *"Too often we drift along from day to today, taking our blessings for granted, until God permits a natural calamity to occur and remind us of our total dependence on Him."*

A few sentences later he inserted these words which now appear to have been prophecy, *"God didn't have to send great battalions to Judah to bring the people to their knees. All He needed was a swarm of little insects, and they did the job. Sometimes He uses bacteria or viruses so tiny that you need a special microscope to see them...He is 'the Almighty' and none can stay His powerful hand."*

Written twenty-four years ago in a chapter titled *'The Day of the Lord'* these words suggest Wiersbe anticipated a virus that would call for **transformation.** He states that "Day of the Lord" was used frequently by prophets to describe "local calamities" that were "a precursor to worldwide judgment."[20]

There is a need for immediate **transformation.** This will require that we who are patriots today follow the Founders' model and pledge lives, resources and reputation to change from a culture living for power and pleasure to living to love God and our neighbors.

The first step—repentance.

"Most merciful God,
We confess that we have sinned against you
in thought word and deed,
by what we have done,
and by what we have left undone.
We have not loved you with our whole heart;
we have not loved our neighbors as ourselves.
We are truly sorry and we humbly repent.
For the sake of (source of your individual belief),
Have mercy on us and forgive us;
that we may delight in your will,
and walk in your ways,
to the glory of your Name. Amen."[21]

---

[20] *Be Amazed, OT Minor Prophets,* p. 67 by Warren Wiersbe, published by David C. Cook 1996
[21] Book of Common Prayer, 1977

The next step—ask for Holy Spirit wisdom, direction, courage, and power in order to serve in the transformation process.

A close friend lived this motto, "Always leave it better than when you found it." We have work to do if this will be true for our progeny. Joshua two thousand years ago said it clearly,[22]

> "But if serving the Lord seems undesirable to you, then choose for yourselves this day whom you will serve…But as for me and my household, we will serve the Lord."

How to be obedient to The Greatest Commandment?

1. Repent
2. Ask for Holy Spirit wisdom, direction, and courage.

---

[22] Joshua 24:15

Today's Lax List

Disobedience to God's word is the norm today among those who call themselves Christians. What might God do regarding a people lax in following scriptural teachings including:

- Loving God,
- Loving one another,
- Ten commandments,
- Protecting the most vulnerable,
- Weekly worship habits,
- Giving God credit,
- Seeking God's will,
- Recognizing and using spiritual gifts,
- The Great Commission,
- Tithing,

- Trusting God,
- Thanking God for blessings,
- Parenting, and
- Marital fidelity?

It is time to make the "Lax List" a "Virtue List."

- It takes a passion to override a passion. Our present "power and pleasure" passion, is powerful.
- Agape love, God's love is all-powerful. The Founders relied on Nature's God to defeat the most powerful army in the world. This power is still available to give victory.
- What must we do? Have a passion to obey His Commandments.

A Final Word

The writing of this commentary was completed two days before Independence Day. 244 years earlier our Founders pledged their lives, fortunes and sacred honor to become independent from the most powerful country in the world thereby creating, quoting Lincoln, *"a new nation, conceived in liberty and created to the proposition that all men are created equal."* This is our heritage, a heritage that provided the foundation for this country to become the most powerful country in the world.

Lincoln went on to say *"Now we are engaged in a great civil war testing whether that nation, or any nation so conceived and so dedi-*

cated, can long endure." Now we are engaged in a great war testing our nation. Our war may be against a plague, Covid-19, but it is just one more in a long string of disasters that keep coming and coming. Is it not time to explore so called-acts of God; is it not time to realize this is God's world, we are his caretakers and we are here to obey his commandments.

Our lives, fortunes and sacred honor are on the line. What legacy do we want to leave, living for self or living lives that love God and neighbors? Stop and think about that.

The Introduction to this commentary asked this question, "How do we get back to life that is fun, fulfilling, and meaningful?" Does the "I, me, mine" path get us there?

Or was the Creator not spot on when he said the greatest thing you can do with

your life is to love me wholeheartedly
and love your neighbor as yourself?

About the Author

Raised on an Illinois dairy farm, Jim Dickson joined the U.S. Army paratroopers after high school and then earned an undergraduate degree in political science and history, and a law degree from the University of Illinois. His wife of 67 years, Peggy is a Wellesley College history major graduate. Her early years were spent in China where her father was a medical missionary. Jim and Peggy worked in faith mission for thirty years serving churches in the U.S. and Eastern Europe in the areas of discipleship and evangelism. They have five children and fifteen grandchildren.

Jim's writings primarily relate to our Founding Fathers faith, family traditions

and values, and applying biblical principles to daily life.